The Chosen Puppy

How to Select and Raise a Great Puppy from an Animal Shelter

• • •

CAROL LEA BENJAMIN

HOWELL BOOK HOUSE

New York

For Mimi Kahn,
my real and chosen sister

Macmillan General Reference
A Simon & Schuster Macmillan Company
1633 Broadway
New York, NY 10019-6785

Library of Congress Cataloging-in-Publication Data
Benjamin, Carol Lea.
   The chosen puppy: how to select and raise a great puppy from an animal
shelter/Carol Lea Benjamin.
      p.   cm.
   ISBN 0-87605-417-3
   1. Dogs.   2. Puppies.   I. Title.
SF427.B5176   1990
636.7—dc20   89-29081   CIP

20 19 18 17 16 15 14 13 12 11

Printed in the United States of America

Contents

Acknowledgements

For running trials of the Puppy Evaluation Test and offering valuable feedback, my sincere gratitude to:

The American Society for the Prevention of Cruelty to Animals, New York, New York:
Sue Sternberg, Coordinator of Pet-Assisted Therapy, Micky Niego, Coordinator of Companion Animal Services and Victoria Halboth, volunteer.

Atlanta Humane Society, Atlanta, Georgia:
Katey Breen, Director of Education and Public Relations.

Marie Ehrenberg, Dog Behavior Consultant, Rochester, Minnesota.

Greenfield Area Animal Shelter, Greenfield, Massachusetts:
Joyce E. Karpinski, Executive Director, Denise Ostroski, Shelter Manager, Angela Nickerson, volunteer,
in conjunction with:
Northampton Dog Obedience Training School:
Jeanne Kowaleski, Instructor, and assistants Ann Carey, Ann Marie Foley, Madeline Heon and Mary Neill.

The Henry County Humane Society, Kewanee Chapter, Kewanee, Illinois:
Maryann Akers-Hanson, journalist, Erica Hanson, volunteer and Karen Rogula, volunteer.

The Noah's Ark Animal Welfare Association, Inc., Ledgewood, New Jersey: Barbara Dyer, Executive Director and Nicola Redmond, Manager.

The Ramapo Kennel Club, Ramapo, New Jersey.

Washington County Humane Society, Slinger, Wisconsin: Phyllis Cook, Director, Pat Sullivan, Dog Obedience Trainer and Andrea Gripentrog, adopter.

I am grateful, too, to Micky Niego and Sue Sternberg for reading the manuscript and each making excellent suggestions for improvements, to Bobbi Giella for her enthusiasm and generous sharing of resource materials, to Stephen Zawistowski, Ph.D., Vice President of Education, the A.S.P.C.A., for expanding my knowledge of the animal kingdom beyond dogs, to Job Michael Evans for helping me transform my insecurities and troubles into stand-up comedy, and to some others I couldn't do without—my publisher, Sean Frawley (Man of the Year in my book), my friend and editor, Seymour Weiss, my smart, terrific agent, William Reiss and my darling husband, Stephen Lennard.

Hugs for my friends at Annabel's for the best scones anywhere and for good buddies Martin Bluford and Cara White.

For going above and beyond the call of duty, my gratitude again to Sue Sternberg who, in helping me simplify, clarify and improve the Puppy Evaluation Test, got trampled, ignored, peed on, scratched and bitten. Thanks, Sue.

And a kiss for Oliver. I still miss you, Red.

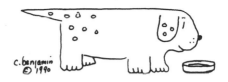

Introduction

ON PRINCIPLE I knew I would like this book. Some fifteen million animals are received by shelters and pounds every year and approximately half this number are dogs. This makes the shelter the most logical place to go to find the ideal puppy, dog, kitten or cat for many reasons. Not only is the selection extraordinary, but the support services that many shelters give—careful medical exams, behavioral counseling, a free spay or neuter operation when the animal matures and much appreciation from the shelter staff for rescuing an otherwise unwanted animal—are extraordinary. And the price of the animal is usually very low.

After reading *The Chosen Puppy*, however, I liked this book for what it does. In a very readable and not too long text, nicely sprinkled with humorous and very helpful drawings, we learn a lot about puppies—and mature dogs as well.

And that's important, because animal shelters typically have many more mature dogs available than they have puppies. I, myself, prefer adopting an older dog, for if you approach your examination of the animal in the manner that Carol Benjamin outlines here, you not only can learn much about the dog's temperament, intelligence and health, but you also know what you have in size and activity level. When carefully evaluated, what you see is what you get.

But while shelters have many, many older dogs, most people who come to shelters and want a dog typically first want to look at the puppies. Or even when they don't, the first puppy they see usually changes their minds. Since any shelter worth the name carefully screens potential adopters in order to determine whether they would be responsible caretakers of the animal they would like to adopt (and even screens them to determine what kind of an animal they should adopt), the best of intentions on the part of an adopter can go awry if emotions are in charge of the adoption process. And even when emotions are not dominant, intelligent choices can still be frustrated if you don't know what to look for, how to choose and what should be avoided given your lifestyle and home environment.

Not only is this straightforward, to-the-point and delightfully written book as useful to those wanting to share their lives with dogs as it is to those willing to devote the time and energies needed to properly acclimate puppies to their homes, but it is also good reading for those who already have pet dogs. Running the busiest animal shelter program in the country, I fully understand the importance of a bond beneficial to both the human and the animal. Here you understand why it is important to neuter your pet, and how beneficial daily grooming of your puppy and dog is—for you, as well as for him. What is said about feeding your puppy or dog is right on target, as are the extremely helpful rudiments of training that every dog must experience. Proper behavioral training goes hand in hand with learning how to communicate with your dog, and the communication tips given here will prove extremely helpful.

Simply put, start turning the pages, for you're going to like this book a lot and the joys and happiness unique to a relationship with your "chosen puppy" will be even greater for you in the future.

John F. Kullberg, Ed.D.
President
The American Society for the
Prevention of Cruelty to Animals

1

From Shelter Puppy to Chosen Puppy

HE IS HARDLY ever handled by a loving human being. No one has the time.

He cannot play with others of his own kind (the way a puppy learns how to grow up to be a dog). It might spread disease.

He spends his babyhood with nowhere to relieve himself but the very area in which he must also eat and sleep.

Unloved, he waits. He will probably wait for nothing.

But this little dog could become a devoted and loving pet. *You* can make the difference.

The little puppy in the shelter will not grow up to be another Rin Tin Tin or Lassie. He may be every bit as smart and loyal. He may be protective, learn tricks, become a movie star. After all, Benji is not a purebred dog. So, in fact, your shelter puppy could grow up to be another Benji. But what he will not do is be guaranteed to grow up to be a certain size and look a certain way. Few shelter puppies are purebred. So if you must have a Bulldog or a Beagle, have one. In this case, a shelter puppy is not for you.

Perhaps the exact look of the dog who could be your best friend is not an important issue. After all, it's what's inside that really counts. Inside, the shelter puppy is pure dog. He can be as sweet, as willing to please, as playful, as affectionate, as smart, as loyal as any dog whose breed you can name. And what's more, he's unique, drawing his many fine qualities from not just one but a variety of breeds. His looks will be unique, too. He's his own pup, one of a kind.

So if what you want is the kind of love and friendship that only a dog can deliver, a shelter puppy might be perfect for you. When you get home every day, no matter what kind of day it has been, he'll be waiting, overjoyed to see you. He's the dog to take long walks with, to take care of, the dog who'll never be too busy or too tired or too cranky or distracted to give you all his attention.

More than that, you think that some of the way we have come to live in this world is all wrong. We humans have become sloppy with our environment, trashing it wherever we go. We pollute our waters with toxic wastes. We lay waste the land with strip mining. We defoliate the forests. We are heartless to the animals we share this earth with, as if we had all the rights and they had none. We treat pet dogs like so many soda cans, simply tossing them away when they are of no more use or interest to us.

Animal shelters have evolved to clean up our mess, to try to find homes for the precious life that no one will take responsibility for, to offer the others a painless death. If you think about it, the system stinks.

If this bothers you, maybe you want to do something about it. Of course, you're only one person. You cannot right the world. But you can make it right for one puppy. You can take what someone else considered trash, this precious, living thing, and turn it into gold. You can take the disappointment out of one puppy's eyes. You can make it so that one puppy waited for a reason, not for naught. He won't be just a statistic in the grim work shelters do for us. He'll become a great and loving pet, your pet, and just as you were there for him, he'll be there for you—always.

Should you give your heart and a home to a waiting shelter puppy? If you are looking for a dog to love who will love you back and that dog need not be a purebred dog, of course you should. While a shelter puppy, a dog of uncertain ancestry, will not give you the comfort of knowing in advance his adult look, size and probable temperament, there is an awful lot you can determine. This book will show you how—how to choose a healthy, trainable, sweet-tempered puppy, how to raise and train your puppy so that he will grow up to be the loyal, wonderful pet you deserve, how to meet the special needs of a puppy who has spent time in a shelter.

WHAT EVERY PUPPY NEEDS—AND THEN SOME

The shelter puppy needs what every other puppy needs. Only in this case, he may not have gotten it all. But the dog is a dynamic and forgiving creature. He learns. He relearns. He heals. Armed with knowledge and your generous heart, you can give the little puppy adopted from an animal shelter what he missed—and more—so that his life with you will be a rich and happy one.

The shelter puppy, as every puppy, needs to be socialized. Perhaps he sat alone for a time before you chose him. Chapter 4 contains a program you can use to give him more confidence with new people, in new places and with other pets.

The shelter puppy will need to be trained. What puppy doesn't? Using this book as your guide, you will see just how trainable he is, even before you bring him home. Chapters 5, 6, 7 and 8 contain an easy-to-follow training course for shelter puppies.

Your shelter puppy will need good food, grooming, some time to rest and a time to play with others of his own kind. And if you find he needs more work, more patience, more time than some ordinary puppy, perhaps, then, you'll get more love in return.

You can decide to make a difference—just you. You really can. You can choose to go to the shelter and save a little puppy, to give him love and care and keep him safe from harm. You can choose to perform an ecologically sound act. Rather than destroy or ignore, you can save and nourish.

With the help of this book, you will learn how to communicate with a puppy, how to bring out his charm, how to understand what you see so that you will be able to choose the best puppy for your own temperament, the right puppy for you. You will learn how to test a puppy, to see if he has the potential to become a satisfying pet, to see if he's outgoing, good with your children, easy to train, affectionate. And then you will choose the very best puppy for you.

He may have been discarded along with his mother and his

littermates. No one had bothered to spay her or keep her on a leash. The miracle of birth was pretty interesting, but then, rather quickly, they all become too much trouble.

He may have been born on the street...

He may have been born on the street or behind someone's garage. Or perhaps the puppy you like best had a home for a month or two. But he cried at night. Or they moved and didn't bother to take him along. Or he made a mess on the rug. And no one had the time to educate him. Instead, they threw him away.

He may have been in the shelter for a while, two or three weeks, or more. Maybe he's a little shy now, afraid of people. Maybe he's afraid of other dogs, too. He may never have walked on pavement or stepped on carpeting, never been on a leash. Possibly he's had no education, no training, no limits set, no freedom. He may have hardly ever been held. He may never have fallen asleep on someone's lap.

Despite his humble beginnings, he's no second-rate citizen. Once you step in, he becomes a chosen puppy, forever special, in the way adopted children are. You have thoughtfully selected the right thing to do. Now you will choose just the right puppy. You will step forward and make a difference. Because of you, one puppy's wait will not be in vain.

Or he made a mess on the rug.

C. benjamin
© 1990

Because of you, one puppy's wait will not be in rain.

2

How to Talk
to a Puppy

THERE ARE THREE WAYS to insure clear communication with the puppy you are about to take into your home and heart.

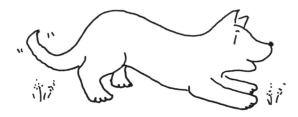

First, you can learn to understand the natural puppy by becoming aware of how a puppy perceives the world.

Second, you can learn to understand canine body language, the way in which your dog communicates with other dogs and will communicate with you, if you will let him.

Third, you can teach the puppy a little of your own spoken language via invitations, commands, praise and corrections.

UNDERSTANDING THE NATURAL PUPPY

Untamed and without people in his life, the natural dog would live in a loose family grouping or *pack*. Each pack would have its own territory where it would live and hunt and raise its young. The pack would protect this territory against other packs of the same species, the competition. And each pack would have a leader, an *alpha* male or female to make all the important decisions, to be listened to, to keep the peace, to be followed and adored by the others.

In order to protect the pack against overpopulation during lean times, the alpha dog would be the only one to mate and sire or bear offspring. This is an important thing to keep in mind if you have any concerns about neutering your pet.

In practice, an alpha animal would rarely have to fight to defend his position. Instead, the top dog would indulge in rituals that would be understood by all the others, rituals that would remind the others that he was in charge. He might stare at a lesser dog—only he is "allowed" direct eye contact—or he might toss a dog over on its back, even bare his fangs and "pretend" to grab it by the throat. But as long as the other dog would follow the script, expose his neck, avert his eyes, stay on his back without struggling until the "confrontation" was over, no one would get hurt. These rituals only *look* violent. In reality, they are not. They are, instead, communication.

Dog, and wolves, can sometimes spot an alpha animal even from a distance, with no ritual performed. They sense the quiet strength, the authority, the confidence. After all, the concept of *alpha* has always been a part of their lives. When they were small and defenseless whelps, someone wonderful and all-knowing took care of all their needs, protected them, loved and taught them. The first alpha in every dog's life is his mother, a perfect model for what is to come—a firm, fair owner who will provide leadership, protection, food and love.

Of course, your puppy is not a wild dog. He's a domesticated animal. He is not capable of living on his own, as his wild ancestors were. Yet he understands pack structure and pack rules. This means he needs, and is capable of accepting, your leadership. You, and every member of your family—your dog's new mixed-species pack—must be higher ranked than your dog. This will keep the peace, help prevent biting and keep your dog as secure as he felt with his mother.

How will you become alpha to your dog? The natural way, by ritual. Here are some paths to alpha that are clear, gentle and humane:

Teach your dog basic obedience. (Instructions follow in chapters 5, 6, 7 and 8.)

Always praise when he is good.

Always correct when he is naughty.

Teach your dog good manners. Chapter 6 will show you how.

Use a long down stay (chapter 7), once a day, as a nonviolent way to restrain your dog. This reminds him that you are in charge.

Be consistent.

Be fair, confident, humane and loving. (His mother was.)

All the exercises and training in this book will help establish your position as a benevolent leader in your dog's eyes.

The natural puppy is a pack animal, born to play a serious game of follow the leader. Now your family is his pack. You will live together and share food, shelter, work and fun. In order to do that smoothly, you will need to be able to read his body language. Here's what it looks like.

THE BODY LANGUAGE OF DOGS

Friendly

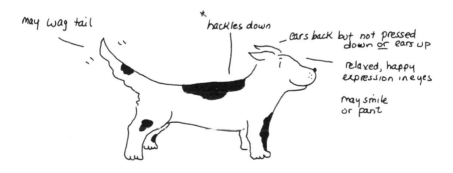

may wag tail

*
hackles down

ears back but not pressed
down or ears up

relaxed, happy
expression in eyes

may smile
or pant

* hackles : guard hairs on the neck
and back which stand up
when a dog is afraid or
angry.

The Play Bow
An invitation to play

tail may wag! " "

rear up

rump may wiggle

eyes dancing

bright, friendly expression
may pant

front paws down

Fearful or Shy

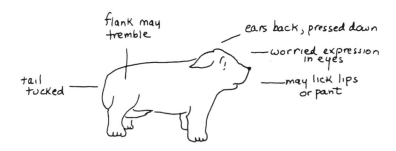

flank may tremble

ears back, pressed down

worried expression in eyes

may lick lips or pant

tail tucked

Investigative with other dogs
Dogs take turns sniffing

the other dog "freezes"

One dog sniffs

Assertive, Aggressive

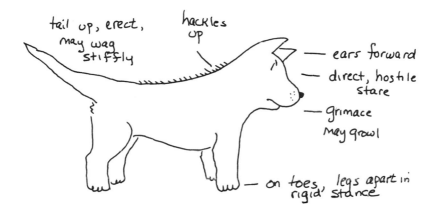

tail up, erect, may wag stiffly

hackles up

— ears forward
— direct, hostile stare
— grimace
  may growl

— on toes, legs apart in rigid stance

You can use body language, too. Stand tall and use your deepest voice when training; bend or crouch and become less assertive, more equal, for play.

Stand tall when training...

Crouch when playing.

TEACHING YOUR PUPPY TO UNDERSTAND YOU

From the very first day you bring your new friend home, you will be learning to understand his language and you will be teaching him to understand *your* language. First of all, you will give him a name. After that, you will use a brief vocabulary list, perhaps the one that follows or a similar one, so that you can invite him to join you, let him know he's good or naughty, play some games, give commands and, in general, have good communication. Here is a sample vocabulary list you can use with your chosen puppy:

Vocabulary for a Chosen Puppy.

Sit, Down, Stand, Stay, Come, Heel. Basic obedience commands.

Okay. Use to break a command.

No. Use to stop an action the dog should never do, e.g., nipping.

GOOD dog. Use to praise.

BAD dog. Use to correct.

Take it. Use in retrieving games.

Out. Use when dog should release what he has retrieved—or stolen.

Off. Use when dog is on the couch.

Speak. Use when you want the dog to bark.

Enough. Use when you want the dog to stop an action the dog may sometimes do, e.g., barking.

Now that you can communicate with a puppy, it's time to go to the shelter and make your selection.

3

Choosing the Best Puppy for *You*

YOU GOT THE MESSAGE and you're psyched. Next Saturday you're going to the shelter and you're going to fall in love. In no time you'll be walking out the door with a puppy whose life you have saved, your own chosen puppy.

Please note well. Don't fall in love until *after* you have found the right puppy for *you*. The right puppy is one who is lively, but not a maniac, loving, but not maudlin or clingy, zestful but still trainable, showing an appropriate attitude with dogs as well as people and he is most definitely a puppy who is sound and healthy.

In order to find *your* right puppy, plan on several trips to the shelter, assuming that it will take both careful consideration and time to locate the perfect puppy for your family. Before you make your choice, be smart and even a little hard-hearted. This is the time to be a careful shopper. Before you let yourself fall deeply and madly in love, make sure you have selected the dog that has the right temperament for your family, one that you have tested to make sure it is educable and can recover from its stay in an institution in a relatively short time frame, one that is reasonably socialized, of the right age to be adopted (you are going to do some background checking here) and one that is at least healthy looking—no runny eyes, no dull, dry coat, no crusty nose. A healthy, sound dog is work enough. A sickly pup or one with a poor temperament is close to impossible.

So don't, in an attempt to right the world, rush out and adopt the most pitiful creature ever to slink across the face of the earth because you feel so sorry for it. You do not get extra points for adopting the worst puppy in the shelter. When this poor wretch doesn't work out and you bring it back to the shelter, it has even less of a chance than it did the day you took it.

Don't take the boldest, most dominant puppy either, not unless you've had scads of dogs, assertive ones, and trained them all impeccably. The most dominant puppy will grow up to be the most dominant dog—difficult to train, bossy, apt to become a biter.

You will not be doing anyone a favor—not the puppy, not the shelter, not your family, not yourself—by selecting the wrong puppy to adopt. If you adopt a puppy who is too shy, too aloof, too aggressive, too active, too damaged or too sickly, you'll probably end up bringing him back. You might feel guilty about your failure, frustrated that it didn't work out or even angry at the puppy for being so difficult despite all your time and effort. You might feel heartbroken, too, and afraid to try again, even with a more suitable puppy.

What about this puppy you return to the shelter when it doesn't work out? Who will want him now that he's grown big and clumsy, now that he's lost some of his puppy cuteness and learned some bad habits as well? Adopting the wrong puppy could mean ruining that pup's chance for a good, stable home as well as destroying your own willingness to provide a home for some sweet dog you have yet to meet.

Given the grim fact that there are thousands upon thousands more dogs and puppies than good homes for them, you can and should be choosy. After all, if you select an appropriate puppy, nothing on earth could make you bring him back! Instead, you'll live happily with him for many, many years to come. For your own sake as well as for the puppy's, give this relationship the best possible chance for success. Toward this end, when you visit the local shelter, before you even look at the puppies, be sure to enlist the aid of the shelter workers, adoption counselors or whoever is available who knows what different people need in a pet and who is also familiar with all the available puppies. Remember, too, that a puppy you adopt will become a member of your family, so the whole family should be in on the selection, especially the children. In this way, you will see for yourself whether or not a given puppy relates well to *all* the members of your family *before* you take him home.

c.benjamin © 1990

The puppy you adopt will become a member of your family.

Perhaps you are wondering what breeds so endearingly combined to create this unique individual you are about to call your own. You can't always tell. Some dogs are clearly Shepherd mixes, part Beagle or terrier types. Others are the product of generations of mixed-breed dogs, the dedicated mutts. But even when the look of a dog seems to give a clue about his heritage, there's no way to be certain which instincts will be dominant.

This is why the *Puppy Evaluation Test* is so important. It will demonstrate to you those personality traits that can make or break a relationship between a person and a dog. It will show you how active the dog is, if he's gentle or not, how trainable he is, if he's people-centered. After all, if a pup is noisy, does it matter that he's noisy because he's part terrier? Or is the issue rather this: how much barking can you live with and is this puppy trainable so that you can modify his bent to bark? Remember, no matter what breed he *appears* to be, a noisy puppy is likely to grow up to be a noisy dog.

If a puppy looks like a Collie mix or has lots of terrier in him, like Benji, don't pigeonhole the little guy without testing him first. There are guarding types who couldn't care less, laid-back herding dogs, quiet terriers. And don't forget, there's also obedience training, which won't change the fabric of your dog but will give you some control.

FIRST STEPS FIRST

Before you get to look at any puppies, a trained volunteer or employee at the shelter will probably want to interview *you* to determine whether or not you could give a puppy a good home and, if so, what kind of a puppy would be best for you. You can help this process along by having thought out in advance how active a dog you'd like. Do you jog, do you take long hikes or are you a couch potato? What size dog would you be comfortable with? Remember that even after you train your dog, he may want to go left when you want to go right. How much grooming can you handle? Bathing and brushing, plucking, stripping, combing knots and mats out of a long coat take time and can be hard work. How much time can you devote to (*a*) your dog and (*b*) his obedience training? Some types are more assertive, more stubborn, more willful and take more time to train.

Before you go to the shelter, consider what age puppy would fit into your lifestyle. Puppies under three months of age (these will still have all their baby teeth) cannot be left alone for long periods of time. If you want a young puppy, someone must be at home, at least for the first couple of months. Puppies three to four months of age (these have their adult teeth on top, front only) can be left alone for a few hours at a time. You could manage with a puppy over three months of age if you work part-time or if you can get someone to come in during the day to take care of the puppy for an hour or so. Puppies four to five months old (these have adult teeth top and bottom, front only) can manage the day alone if you get a dog walker to come in once while you are gone. Like babies, puppies have many needs. They should not be isolated. So if you are out all day or very busy in general, an adult dog might be a better choice for you.

All these factors should come up during your interview. Once you have gotten approval and are invited to see the puppies, you'll need some rules and guidelines to help you choose the best puppy for you.

Rule 1 Do not fall in love with a sick puppy.

The very first thing you are going to do is weed out obviously sick puppies. Unless you have your veterinarian with you, you will not know everything about the health of the little puppies who are waiting to be adopted. All you can do for now is eyeball the puppies and select from the soundest of those available for adoption. Then, after questioning, testing and selecting, the very first place you will go is to the veterinarian of your choice. Only after he or she has given the puppy a clean bill of health will you really fall in love. Minor problems are okay, of course. After all, who's perfect? But don't adopt a pup with a major health problem. It could break your heart.

Look at the puppy's eyes. They should be clear and shiny. They should not be crusty or running.

Check the puppy's nose. The nose does not have to be cold and wet, but it should not be running or crusty either.

Check the puppy's teeth. White teeth are healthy. Stained teeth are not and could be a result of serious illness.

Check the puppy's coat. The hair should look and feel healthy. Puppy coats often don't shine—the coat tends to be woolly on many puppies. But the hair should be thick and alive. Look out for bald patches, thin, greasy or dry, dead-looking coats. They could signal potential trouble.

bright eyes, not runny

rose not runny or crusty

moves well, not lame

white teeth

healthy coat, no bald patches

Choose a healthy puppy.

Try to see if the puppy moves as if it is sound, remembering all along that young animals are not sure on their feet. Do not select a puppy who is lame.

While you're still looking at the physical puppy, ask about the probable adult size of these puppies. The size of a puppy's feet is *not* accurate in predicting how big he'll eventually be! But sometimes the shelter workers know how big the mother was and, far less frequently, how big the father was. With some questioning and careful observation, you shouldn't end up with a Saint Bernard mix when what you really wanted was a part Chihuahua.

I have always favored big dogs, but now, for the first time, I have a small dog. Now I know that good things come in small packages, too, and that sometimes it's very handy to have a pet you can lift up. The amount of love a dog can give has nothing whatsoever to do with his size. Big or small, they are all real dogs. So be practical. Choose a dog who you will be able to handle when he's fully grown.

Rule 2 Ask about temperament testing and get a history.

At this point you can ask the adoption counselor if the shelter does any type of temperament testing. The results of these tests can help you figure out which puppies might be suitable for you and your family. Some shelters test their puppies to discover which are too assertive, too aloof or too shy to make good pets. These results can tell you how quickly and well your puppy will bond to you and how difficult or easy your puppy will be to train. In temperament testing, the test is usually done once and the puppy is assessed on his performance at that time. If the shelter you visit does testing, they can explain in detail what the test is and what it reveals about the puppies.

Once you are presented with a choice of appropriate puppies, you can select three or four candidates that you will test with the help of the adoption counselor (see Rule 3). Before you test them, however, request a history on each of these little dogs. See if you can find out how old each puppy was when it was removed from its mother, then its litter mates. THIS IS VERY IMPORTANT. A puppy who has not had enough time with its mother (at least three weeks) and its littermates (at least five or six weeks) might never act like a normal dog.

Some professionals will take a young orphan and give it foster care, hoping that they will be able to provide the contact, stimulation, frustration and full variety of experience that will allow this dog to act appropriately with both dogs and people as it grows to adulthood. I strongly advise you *not* to do this. Do not take a puppy under six weeks of age. Raising a normal puppy is hard work. The fostered puppy will be even more work, with no guarantee that after the enormous time and effort you put in, it will ever act like a normal dog.

It is from his mother and littermates that a little dog learns how to play nicely, how to mouth instead of biting hard, how to wait his turn, how to stand up for himself, how to be social and charming, how to be a puppy and then a dog. Without these models and these lessons, a puppy can turn out to be antisocial and fearful. He often becomes a biter. He rarely can play well with other dogs. These are not small problems.

There will be more than enough puppies from which you can choose, so please choose one who is most likely to become a great pet and your lifelong friend.

Rule 3 Ask if you can test the puppies you like.

After you have narrowed down the field to three or four favorite, healthy-looking puppies, ask if you can test the puppies one at a time to see which would be the best for you to adopt. The purpose of this test is somewhat different from the usual temperament testing and so is the method used.

Have you ever had to stay in a hospital? Do you remember coming home, even after only a few days away, and finding that everything looked peculiar to you? Things seemed too large or too small. Everything looked unreal. Even familiar noises sounded strange and different.

Puppies, too, react to time in an institution. Even in the best, cleanest, most humane shelter, puppies may get a case of "shelter shock." They cannot receive the same amount of loving care they would have in a good home. In many shelters, the employees just don't have the time to pet and carry around all the puppies so that they can get used to handling and affection. Puppies may be deprived of the kind of stimulation, handling and variety they would get in a loving home. The puppy you like may never have had the opportunity to walk on grass, carpeting or even linoleum. He may have been alone instead of with littermates. He may hardly ever have been handled by people and he may be fearful of them at first. However, if he can demonstrate quick recovery from "shelter shock," he will probably make a fine pet. This test checks the ability to recover, the ability to relearn, the ability to forgive and forget a deprived past.

Unlike temperament testing (Puppy Aptitude Testing), this new test (Puppy Evaluation Testing) is not designed to be tried once. What you will do is note the puppy's initial behavior and instead of judging the puppy by what he does at first, you will note what he does given several tries and judge him on what you learn about him during this process.

The primary goal of this test is to evaluate the potential of any given puppy to become a good pet. It will help if you keep two things in mind. First, the fact that the acronym for the Puppy Evaluation Test is PET is not an accident. Second, one of the meanings of the word *pet* is favorite.

Please be aware that no test will give you the definitive answer on which puppy you should adopt. The Puppy Evaluation Test is designed to be one of several factors that will help you see if your favorite puppy will make a good pet. It will help you to make an educated guess about which pups might be appropriate pets for your family.

Here is the thinking behind the test. Suppose your favorite puppy has spent most of his young life in his cage. When he comes out, everything is new to him. He has not had the chance, so far, to try new surfaces under his feet, to meet and greet lots of new people, to use his mind to learn words, to attach himself to a person. When you put him on the floor, he might just freeze. He might not come to you. He might be scared stiff.

This puppy won't look like a great candidate for you. However, suppose you bend down and call him, and after a minute, he gets brave and comes. You pet him, move away and try again. This time, he doesn't think it over for quite as long. This time he only takes a minute to come, and see, his tail is up. He's less frightened. And the third or fourth time you bend down and whistle to him, he runs in, his little tail wagging. This puppy is demonstrating that he can recover quickly from his deprived beginning. He is showing you that he has the capacity to learn, to grow, to begin to trust. If he does as well on all his tests, this puppy will make a good pet.

Here's the best part. Suppose you find a little puppy who looks all shiny and healthy and shows quick recovery, some learning and even becomes fairly outgoing when you test him. Chances are this is not merely an okay puppy, he's a great puppy. After all, it's pretty easy to be trusting and friendly and to learn rapidly when you've had all the advantages, when everything in your young life has been nearly perfect. But a puppy who can shine after being deprived may have an extra special resiliency, an extra dose of what it takes to survive and thrive. When *this* little dog comes up roses, you've got yourself one swell dog.

Following are some simple tests you can use to see how flexible, educable and forgiving any prospective puppy might be. *Be sure to test each puppy by itself without the distraction of other puppies or dogs in the room.* Do not worry about doing the test perfectly. Your only concern is to learn enough about each puppy to make an appropriate choice. And don't think of this as pass-fail for each puppy. A puppy who may be wrong for you may be perfect for someone else.

THE PUPPY EVALUATION TEST

1. Does the puppy react well to a new environment?

Take the puppy you are considering to a quiet area and place him down on the floor. He may need a little time to get used to a new surface, new smells and a larger area. He may also, once out of a small cage, relieve himself several times. Of course, you'll clean up after him. It's not only the right thing to do. It's good practice.

Note how the puppy reacts to a new environment. The speed with which he begins to explore will let you know how flexible he is, how quickly he'll adjust to your home. If the puppy freezes at first, but then begins to explore and get friendly, this is excellent.

However, if the puppy never moves from the spot where he was placed or runs away and tries to hide, this is not the puppy to adopt. Nor is the puppy who runs you down, climbing up on you and biting, the one to take home. But the puppy who can get comfortable in a new environment within a few minutes, who begins to check things out and, better still, begins to play, is definitely a candidate.

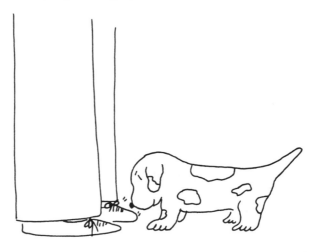

Is he curious? Does he explore, sniff around? Does he begin to play?

Now ask yourself the following question: does this puppy approach a new environment with curiosity and confidence?

2. Will the puppy come when you call him?

Bend down and sweetly call the little puppy. Stay put, but you can attract the puppy by whistling, clapping your hands, clicking your tongue. If the puppy comes, note how quickly and readily it comes, then briefly pet and praise the puppy for coming.

If the puppy won't come, try to entice it by acting like a puppy. Get down on the floor, try panting, try not looking directly at the puppy, even try whining like another puppy.

The puppy who won't come at first but then comes around in a minute or so is a good possible pet for you. Will he do it again? Move to another spot and try again. Now again.

Does he come more readily each time? Is his little tail untucked, held out, wagging?

In general, the more responsive the puppy is, the better. However, if you call and the puppy runs to you and starts nipping at your hands, he might be too aggressive to make a good pet.

Will he come when you call him?

23

Now ask yourself the following question: does this puppy come willingly and happily when called?

3. Does the puppy accept affection?

After the last recall, begin to pet the puppy gently, stroking him softly from head to rump. You can talk to the puppy or not, whatever seems comfortable to you, but do not hold onto him and force him to stay near you.

Does the puppy respond positively, offering himself to you, rolling over on his back, putting his paws on your legs or leaning on you? Does he lick you?

Or does he bite your hands, act dominant or frantic? If at any time during this test, the puppy should bite you, say NO in a very firm voice. Give the puppy a second chance. If he bites again, if he seems aggressive or wild, out of control, do not complete the test. Most untrained puppies nip. They can easily be taught not to do this. But the dominant or aggressive dog will not easily give up this dangerous habit. So if the dog bites hard, stop the test. Even a very young puppy, if he is very dominant, can make you bleed. And a very dominant puppy will be a difficult dog to train. He will not make a good pet for you.

Does the puppy walk off, as if you weren't there at all? He may be too damaged to relate, too aloof or independent.

Does the puppy seem friendly, but only for a second? Does he come, but then leave right away? Does he let you pet him once, and then find something better to do? He may not be a people-centered dog.

Does the puppy urinate when you pet him? This is okay. It simply means he is a submissive puppy who understands clearly that you are top dog.

In order to become a satisfying pet, a dog should be able to accept affectionate handling. Extremely dominant or aloof dogs do not make satisfying pets for most people. A puppy that acts very submissive can become a fine family pet if he tests well in other areas—if he comes, follows and learns. He will outgrow this submissive urination if it is handled in a calm, matter-of-fact way.

Now ask yourself the following question: does this puppy accept and express affection?

24

C.benjamin© 1990

Will he accept affection?

4. Will the puppy follow you?

Stand up and walk around slowly to see if the puppy will follow you. If he won't follow without coaxing, try calling or whistling to get the puppy to do it. Make allowances for the puppy to stop and sniff and to piddle.

If the puppy freezes and will not follow you, he may be too damaged by early separation from his mother or litter, or too under-socialized to make a good pet. If the puppy turns and walks *away* from you, he may be too aloof or independent, or not a people-centered dog. These puppies tend not to become satisfying pets.

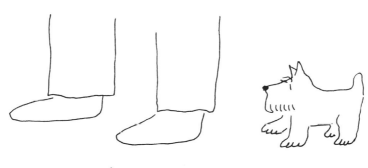

Will he follow you?

Now ask yourself the following questions: is this puppy's general outlook friendly? Does he have much interest in people?

5. Can you teach the puppy to sit?

With the puppy near you, stand up and attract him to look up at you by jingling a set of keys or squeaking a squeak toy over his head. As you do this, tell the puppy, "Sit." Some puppies, when they look up, will lose their balance and have to sit. If the puppy you are testing sits, pet and praise him warmly but calmly, let him follow you a few feet and try the sit again. And twice again.

If the puppy won't sit when he looks up, raise his chin until he sits, or raise his chin as you slide your hand over his back, around his tail and to the place where his hind legs bend. A tiny bit of pressure there will make the puppy sit. Now praise and try again. And twice again.

In four or five tries, if the puppy is "working" and concentrating, he has good aptitude for training. This is very important for a good, easy, fun pet.

Will he sit?

Now ask yourself the following question: is this puppy willing and able to learn?

6. Is this puppy's activity level right for me?

Activity level might just turn out to be the single most important factor that determines how well or poorly you will fare with a given puppy. You may think you want a ball of fire, but think again. Think about how you *really* live—how tired you are after work, how limited your time is, how you long to be left alone to rest, read, watch TV, count clouds. Or on the contrary, are you a nonstop energy machine—do you want a dog who can go the distance with you or keep up with four energetic youngsters? Keep in mind that even if you are a jogger, the puppy can't begin to train with you until he is one year old.

Most families would do best to pick a puppy who seems alive, not overly lively. An extremely lively puppy may need more exercise than you can give him and may be a handful to train. The puppy who is always busy, racing around, never stopping for long, the one who is distracted by anything and everything, always running to check out each new thing—his high activity level does *not* mean he is healthier or stronger than a quieter, less distracted puppy. It simply means he has a high activity level. And he might still be that way when he grows up. An alive puppy simply means a healthy, alert, playful, sound-looking puppy.

You have been with this puppy for several minutes now. Making allowances for the fact that older puppies of three, four and five months of age will be stronger and may run around more than very young puppies of seven to ten weeks of age, rate the puppy's activity level low, medium or high.

Low: Walks, sometimes sits, doesn't always have to be moving.

Medium: Frisky, moves around, trots, occasionally runs, pounces, wiggles.

Is his activity level right for you?

High: Runs continually, pounces, wiggles and paws, always busy.

Now ask yourself the following question: is the puppy's activity level in keeping with my *real* lifestyle?

7. Is this puppy's level of dominance (aggression) appropriate for my family?

The dominant, aggressive dog is the one who doesn't just come up *to* you, he may come up *on* you. When he nears you, he may grab at your hands or your clothes. When you try to get him to sit or when you try to pet him, he may wiggle away. He always tries to take control. He may try to bite you. He may bite hard.

This is a dog that does not accept control easily. Your life with him will always be a struggle. He will not accept you as alpha because he is sure *he* is top dog. Therefore, this is a dog who will not take kindly to "being crossed." He wants his way and he wants it now. He's belligerent, bossy, sassy. When you tell him what to do, he tells you where to go! In other words, he barks back. He is more apt to bite than other dogs. He is less apt to be obedient, well mannered, gentle, good with children. Even a puppy who seems friendly, who wags his tail, who comes when called, can be aggressive. So if the puppy you are testing seems friendly but bites you hard, do not adopt that puppy.

Rate his aggressiveness low, medium or high.

Low: Never nips or mouths, avoids eye contact, is gentle when you handle him.

Medium: Mouths gently, may be frisky and active, but doesn't bite, may fleetingly make direct eye contact, but doesn't stare.

Is he gentle enough for your family?

High: Nips, mouths, bites, runs you down, barks back, gets under foot, always tries to take control, may act wild.

Now ask yourself the following questions: is this puppy's level of dominance appropriate for my family? Will the members of my family be able to handle this puppy?

Scoring the Puppy Evaluation Test

	Response tested	Desired answer
1.	Good reaction to new environment?	yes
2.	Comes when called?	yes
3.	Accepts/shows affection?	yes
4.	Follows?	yes
5.	Shows willingness/ability to learn?	yes
6.	Suitable activity level?	yes
7.	Suitable level of dominance (aggression)?	yes

As you look at the scores, understand that what you do as you raise the puppy will be of paramount importance in how this dog will turn out. You can help a puppy make the most, or the least, of his potential. You can, with the help of this book, help your puppy to become more confident, better able to learn, more capable of express· ing and receiving affection. But this takes time and dedication. And still, you can't work miracles. You probably will not turn that shy dog into a social butterfly or make an easygoing slob out of an overly active, extremely dominant dog.

Since certain things may never change and others may turn out to be too time-consuming or too difficult to do anything about, now is the time to be realistic. The more *desired* answers a puppy has on his score chart, the better chance he has to be a successful pet for you.

Now you have an awful lot of information about one, two or three puppies, all of whom appear to be healthy, trainable, forgiving of a difficult past and not too independent, damaged, aggressive or shy. Now, using what you have learned as well as the charm and eye appeal of these candidates, pick the puppy you think would be best for you. But whatever else you do, do not ignore Rule 4.

Rule 4 Do not fall in love until the veterinarian says you can.

Your little puppy will need protection now, from you and from the care and inoculations the veterinarian will give him. Do not walk him out of the shelter or out on the street. Until such time as he has been fully inoculated, you must carry him. The veterinarian will probably tell you to keep him in. However, if you carry him, you can take him out and about. Take him to visit a friend. Carry him to the mailbox and back. Carry him around the block. It is important for him to see the world so that he doesn't become shy. Then once he has been inoculated, you can begin to walk him on a leash.

You are almost ready to let yourself fall in love, but not just yet. (Remember that there were a few puppies who appealed to you and tested well, just in case.) Now the veterinarian will check your puppy from head to toe. The puppy does not have to be perfect. Who is? If the puppy has some problem that can be easily and completely corrected, it is perfectly fine to make a commitment to him. If, on the other hand, the puppy has had some devastating illness that will effect him negatively in the future, or if he has some terrible problem that cannot be fixed, take him back to the shelter, tell them what you learned and try again with one of the other puppies you liked.

Once the veterinarian pronounces the puppy you like and have tested to be in good health, *now* you can fall in love. At last, you will be taking your chosen puppy home.

4

Puppy Comes Home

NOW THAT HE'S YOURS, you will want a wonderful name for your new puppy. I've known many dogs and most of them had good, plain names like Sam, Max and Jake, endearing names like Sparkle, Star and Woodstock, quirky, people names like Oliver, Ramona, Bubbi and Otis, funny names like Broadway, Salty, Zorro, Zeppo and Arfie.

What's in a name?

There are lots of terrific names for dogs. But one kind of name sometimes seems to backfire. Negative names can cast a shadow on the owner-pet relationship or on the dog itself. That happened to Outlaw, a Doberman. Rascal, Trouble, Evil and Chopper all took their names seriously, too.

So leave Bandit, Fang and Rambo for other people's dogs. When you name your chosen puppy, give him a clever name, an endearing name, a people name, a funny name, any positive image with which to face himself and the world.

What Furnishings Will My Puppy Need?

Here is a basic shopping list for puppy:

Flat or rolled leather collar
Leather or cotton leash, six feet long
Two bowls (stainless steel is best), one for food, one for water
Nail clipper
Wire brush (unless his coat is very short)
Bristle brush
Flea comb
Safe chew toys (rawhide, Nylabone, hard rubber balls)
Dog shampoo
Dog crate (a folding, wire crate in which your puppy will sleep, get housebroken, travel, spend time when you cannot supervise him. See *Where should my puppy sleep?* and chapter 6 for more on how to use the crate.)

What should my puppy eat?

What do you eat? No—I don't mean your puppy should eat people food. He needs dog food. But if you buy your food in the supermarket, you'll probably want to get his food there, too. If you shop at specialized stores, the butcher, the greengrocer, the health food store, you might want to shop at a specialized pet food store for your puppy. Either way, select a dry dog food that offers complete nutrition, is formulated specially for your dog's age and has the lowest levels of preservatives, additives, food coloring and sugar in it. Your puppy can do very well on a diet of dry dog food, a little oil and a supply of fresh water. But if, like me, you like to fuss, he can eat 90 percent dry dog food and 10 percent supplements such as leftover grains and vegetables, leftover meat or chicken or fish (without the bones, please), cottage cheese or yoghurt. Some dogs even enjoy an occasional bite of fruit. This is fine as long as you don't overdo it.

Your little puppy should eat three times a day while he's very young. At about five months old, he can switch to eating twice a day and stay there. Most dogs do best on two meals a day, not one.

Fresh water should always be available, except during early housebreaking when, in order to help make training easier, you can remove the water at about eight in the evening and offer it again in the morning.

Any questions about food? Ask your puppy's veterinarian.

Any questions about food? Ask your puppy's veterinarian.

How often should my puppy get a check-up?

Your puppy should see the veterinarian when you first get him and then every few weeks until his inoculations are completed. After that, unless he's hurt or ill, he should have a complete check-up and booster shots once a year. He will probably also have to see his doctor in the spring for a heartworm test, a simple blood test that is necessary before he can go on heartworm preventative. Prevention, with this and all diseases, is easier and cheaper than allowing the dog to become ill and then trying to cure the illness. Also, ask your veterinarian at what age you should arrange to have your dog neutered. More on this in chapter 6.

How often should my puppy be groomed?

It would be very nice for both you and the puppy if you got into the very pleasant habit of brushing him every day for just a few minutes. It has been discovered that brushing a pet is relaxing for both the pet and the owner, truly relaxing, meaning lower blood pressure and deeper, slower respiration. If you get your puppy used to being handled in this way, it will be easier to train him, to restrain him, to do his nails, to give medication when necessary, to keep him clean, to pet and kiss him. There'll be less loose hair to vacuum up. And, with your hands on your dog like this for a few minutes each day, you won't miss a possible burr, tick, cut, mat or developing skin problem.

During the flea season, use the flea comb, a fine-toothed comb, after each walk to check for fleas and remove them without chemicals. The comb will catch the fleas. By dipping the comb in hot water, you'll remove the fleas from the comb. When you have combed them all out, simply dump the water and fleas into the toilet and flush.

Whenever there is a heavy flea infestation in your area, you may have to step up to flea shampoo, powder or spray. Be sure to read the instructions carefully to make sure the product is safe for the age of your puppy.

Your puppy won't need bathing more than once a month, especially if you brush him daily. While you're at it, check his ears. If they are dirty, clean only where you can see with a clean cloth wrapped around your finger. And once a week, using his own special nail clipper, cut the sharp tip off his toe nails, front and back, including the dewclaw nails which don't wear down by themselves. You may also want to brush his teeth once a week with baking soda and water to prevent tartar build-up and keep his breath fresh.

A grooming routine really doesn't take much time and a sparkling clean dog is a pleasure to be around.

Where should my puppy sleep?

He grew up God knows where—on the street, in a basement, in the shelter. He's a pack animal, born to work and play and eat and sleep with company. So give him yours. Put his crate in your bedroom. This is where your dog should sleep for all his life, *near* you, but not *with* you. Once he's trained, you can leave the crate door open. But even after he's housebroken, he shouldn't sleep in your bed. Doing that would make him feel he was your equal, and eventually, it would make him feel *he* was alpha instead of you.

What's this I hear about my puppy's first night?

Everything you heard is true! Even in your room, your puppy is likely to wake up and cry several times during his first night at home. After all, everything has changed. He's frightened. He doesn't know yet he's in good hands and has a place to stay. You can't tell him that, either. You can only show him, over time, that it's true.

Take heart. In a day or two or three, with your good care, your puppy will begin to feel secure. He's forgiving, isn't he? That's what the puppy test showed. So be patient. When he wakes you, take him to his papers and let him relieve himself. Praise him quickly and return him to his crate. If he has already wet the crate, you'll have to clean it. You may even have to clean *him*. He *must* get in the habit of keeping clean—but he needs time to learn this. Remember that in the shelter, he may have had no choice about where to relieve himself, so this retraining could take time. When he's dry and clean, snug in his crate, go back to bed. But do not take him into bed with you! If you do, you will be training him to wake you every night. Soon enough, he'll sleep through the night. And so will you.

How can I help my puppy build confidence?

Some dogs are born confident. You can see it from the start. You can't help looking at them. They seem to glow.

When you take the confident dog out, everyone makes a fuss. He's got lots of friends. Everyone knows his name. And so his confidence grows.

Some dogs are not all that sure of themselves at first.

Maybe he wasn't top dog in the litter. Or, somehow, he ended up in the shelter. He wasn't handled that much. No one told him he was great or took him places or taught him anything. No one knew his name. In fact, he probably didn't have one.

Now he needs help. This little dog pulls his energy in. It's his way of hiding. You will have to help him learn how to shine.

Does your puppy lack confidence? He loves you, but he sort of disappears or becomes clingy when strangers approach. He takes a while to warm up to kids. Come to think of it, he'd just as soon be off by himself as in a group.

Once he's been inoculated and has learned how to walk on a leash, you can help him build his confidence. Here's how:

Get him out and about. Experience, the successful overcoming of fears, learning how to cope with something new—these things build confidence in a dog. It's hard to create a confident dog by keeping your puppy at home with you. How will he learn that he can march right through his fear of the unknown?

Begin in your own neighborhood, taking your dog for long walks and letting him sniff around, see new things, make new friends. He'll get used to new sounds—children shouting as they play, traffic, bicycle bells, people talking. He'll smell new smells. He'll step on new surfaces. His curiosity will help pull him along. It helps to combat fear.

He'll make new friends.

If your puppy should balk or try to bolt, don't drag him or lose your patience. Bend down and call him to you, praising as he comes. Try a quiet street, then a busier one, then back to a quiet one. Let him build his confidence slowly.

As he comes to enjoy these outings, take him farther from home—to a friend's house, an outdoor circus, a flea market (no jokes, please), a garage sale, an outdoor art show, the park, a dog show, a horse farm. When he's really confident, walk him around downtown on a busy Saturday. Look for new surfaces and offer praise, praise, praise for steady footing on mats, grass, concrete, wood, linoleum, ceramic tile or whatever you can find. Let him know he's a *can-do* pup. How? By experience.

Get him used to noise. Part of being in an institution is the deprivation of home sounds, sights and smells. Does your puppy seem startled when he hears a door slam, your kids yelling, the phone ringing? You can get him used to these sounds and others—the vacuum cleaner, the hair dryer, the television, the dishwasher—with patience and praise.

Never let your puppy run off and hide when a sound spooks him. Never, never pet him to "comfort him" when he is afraid. The petting is reenforcing his spooked behavior by praising him for acting out his fearfulness. Instead, using a collar and leash, put him on a sit stay (see chapter 5). Now patiently repeat the noise and praise the puppy for staying, even when you have to make him stay. Always praise the puppy immediately after the behavior you want—in this case, holding his ground when he hears a strange sound. By appropriate praise that builds confidence, you will be able to help him to become blasé about most household and street noises.

Agility builds confidence. Didn't you take your son to Little League and your daughter to karate lessons (or vice versa) partly to make them more confident? Agility will do the same for your puppy. Look for low obstacles when you are out on your walks. Have your puppy jump low fences, walk on low walls, hop over a broom handle, catch a ball or cookie. And clap for him, too. An extra "That's my pup," never hurt anyone, did it? Remember—don't force, encourage.

Teach him to catch a ball.

A physical accomplishment, as difficult as catching a frisbee or scaling a wall, as simple as learning to feel confident going over a low jump or catching a cookie, these skills will help bring out a dog and make him shine.

Obedience training does the trick. Giving a dog a vocabulary (see chapter 2) and a set of behavior (see chapters 5, 6, 7 and 8) help to make him feel he belongs. When he's in a situation that he finds bothersome, his first big crowd for example, the skill of heeling, the need to pay attention to what he's doing, the praise he gets for his trouble will get him through. Because of his training, he knows how to behave in a new situation. Knowing what to do can help take the fear out of trying something new.

Work does the trick. My German Shepherd, Scarlet, loves to work and amen to that. Wearing saddlebags specially made for dogs, she helps me carry the groceries home. Work makes her feel important and shows her she's a can-do dog, confident, thank you, and loving it.

Your dog can help you out at home, playing with the kids, fetching socks on wash day, carrying the mail.

Some dogs work away from home as well, as therapy dogs, aiding in a miraculous process called pet-assisted therapy. These gentle, obedience-trained, adult dogs, along with their owners, visit people in institutions, stirring warm memories in older people, helping to educate the young, bringing focus and cheer to the mentally or physically disabled. Often the presence of the therapy dogs creates a bridge, allowing otherwise unreachable people to communicate with others, thus enriching their lives. The shelter where you adopt your puppy may be able to tell you how to get involved in pet-assisted therapy. You and your dog will love it.

Work builds muscle, brain power and, yes, confidence.

Exercise does the trick. The lack of exercise looms behind most dog behavior problems. An energetic dog with nothing to do may make his own fun—chewing a pillow, digging a hole, acting like a wild animal instead of a tame one. But a well-exercised dog will be calm. He will be able to concentrate better when you train him. More than that, he'll be well muscled, vigorous, feeling good about himself. It works for people, too. Best for both of you—long, brisk walks. For him, add chasing and retrieving a ball or stick, swimming, playing with other dogs.

Not only is play with other dogs the best exercise your dog can get, the companionship he can get only from his own species is important for his mental health as well. So as soon as he's had all his shots and can safely be around other dogs, find out where the dogs in your area gather to play and give your dog the time of his life. Remember, too, that if you have adopted a social dog and then you never let him play with other dogs, he will lose his friendly, trusting attitude. If you take a shy pup and give him lots of good experiences with other gentle dogs, he may become more sociable. On every level, your dog will grow more confident, will feel better about himself, if he has dog pals with whom to play.

Tricks do the trick. Tricks make people laugh. To a dog, laughter equals praise—as long as you laugh *with* him and not *at* him. Your dog will love to help you create a humorous happening. So here's an easy trick for beginners. More can be found in *Dog Tricks: Teaching Your Dog to Be Interesting, Fun and Entertaining* by Captain Arthur J. Haggerty and Carol Lea Benjamin (Howell Book House, 1982).

READ

Make a sign that says, "Wag your tail." Hold this up in front of your standing puppy and in your highest, friendliest voice say, "Do you want to read this? Good boy, read this sign." And of course your brilliant puppy will read the sign and wag his tail.

What if your puppy is one of those dogs who hardly ever wags his tail? Some dogs don't, even when they're happy. No problem. Just make a sign that says something he will do—"Walk forward," "Put your ears back," "Sit," "Blink," "Bark." And when you say, "Can you read this, pup?" he will. We're tricky—and confidence is what we're after.

If your puppy wasn't born with it, or lost it somewhere along the way, you can give him a little help. Any dog can become more confident—with tricks, with exercise, with work to do, with training and with lots and lots of happy experiences in the larger world away from home.

5

Teaching Your Puppy
How to Learn

A PUPPY has to learn *how* to learn before he can learn commands or even good manners.

Just a few weeks ago, when he was four, five or six weeks old, if he wandered too far from his mother, she'd flatten him to the ground with a paw as if he were Daffy Duck just run over by a steam roller. No one had to translate *that* piece of education. He knew automatically what all her sounds meant—"Watch out!" or "Come here" or "Good puppy." He certainly knew a paw coming down on his neck from a gentle "petting" with her tongue at bath time. He wasn't exactly born yesterday.

But now if you yell and scream because there's a *something* on the rug or if you stand there saying, "Sit, sit, sit," or worse yet, "Sit *down,"* your little dog *won't* know what it's all about. He really won't. He doesn't even know which way to look. But don't lose heart. Here comes the good part.

INTRODUCING A COLLAR AND LEASH

Your first job is to get your puppy used to a collar and leash. Use a buckle collar and praise him when you put it on him. Add a light leash and, holding it loosely, just *follow him* around, praising as you go. In a few days, he'll be ready to *follow you.* Take turns. Keep praising.

TEACHING THE SIT STAY

Once your puppy is used to walking around on leash, begin to teach the sit stay. Use the leash if you need it.

Start out indoors where there's nothing much pulling so hard on that little dog's mind that he can't keep it on you. Remember life when you were a kid—or at least when I was a kid? No TV. Start his training where it's nice and quiet. Let him keep his attention on you. And you keep yours on him.

Take a squeak toy or a ball with a bell in it or a bunch of keys or some crinkly cellophane. Make a little noise right over the dog's head so that he has to look up and as you do this, tell him, "Sit." If you're lucky, he'll look up and in order to keep his balance, he'll *have to* sit. For this you will tell him he is the finest dog ever born. And you'll tell him, "Okay," move to another quiet spot and try it again.

Attract the puppy to look up...

But what if he *doesn't* plant his rear on the wall to wall without so much as a tug on the leash? What if you have a dog who can stand on his hind legs all day long if there's a cute enough toy in sight?

or lift his chin . . .

When he's on all fours, simply lift his chin, *as if* he were looking up, and say, "Sit" as you do so. You can also get a bit more traditional. You can hold firm to the leash and slide your hand *over* the dog's rump and *around* his rear to the back of his legs and, with a tiny bit of pressure there, he'll sit. Praise immediately, warmly and briefly, just the way his mother would have had he responded appropriately to one of her suggestions.

Or pull up on the leash, down over the rump.

Now, working on this simple, gentle sit for a few minutes at a time, over a period of a few days, you're on your way.

Using a leash and working where there are no extraneous distractions, give your sitting dog a slow-motion hand signal as you tell him to stay. The hand signal for *stay* is a flat, open hand, fingers together, palm toward the dog, moved slowly toward the dog's nose as you say the command.

Be patient as you teach. If your little dog breaks ten times, each time say, "No. Sit. Stay," as you place him back where he was, gently. He must cover the same spot. He must face in the same direction. He must be sitting. In fact, when he lies down, and at some point they all do, you can rejoice, but you *still* must immediately get him to sit back up. Laying down means he got the *stay* part. But the point of this is *sit* stay. And the other point of this is that when your puppy truly understands that whoever is holding that leash and saying those words is calling the shots, he will have learned how to learn.

How will you know when you have accomplished the thrilling task of communicating so clearly with another species? Your puppy will look at you.

When you work with most puppies, their eyes will be everywhere but on you. They are looking for the best road out of town. They are looking to escape. In fact, by *deciding* to look at you, your puppy is acknowledging that you are alpha. He is showing that he understands where the next direction is coming from.

What if your puppy turns out to be a hard-nosed type who will give you very early eye contact but whose look won't fit in with the above picture, the decision to look at you as alpha. Your puppy's look is not a look of acceptance, of readiness to be taught more. It may be a look of utter arrogance, a look to see when you might get over this education attack and find something else to do, something he'd approve of. This type of dog may well be a Nordic mix (small pointed ears, double coat, tail curled over back, very independent) or part sight hound (early, calm, direct "stare," built for speed, short coated, tends to be bone thin, couldn't care less). This type of dog might not be so eager to let you be in charge either. So be on the lookout not only for eye contact but for the quality of eye contact you are after.

If you happen to have a hard-nosed, arrogant dog, or a dog who uses his eyes in the direct manner of a sight hound, don't give up. Instead, use alternate clues to tell you when the dog has learned how to learn. Look for signs of relaxation while the dog is on command. My little Shiba Inu will uncurl his tail when on a long down. This signifies his intention to stay rather than break. If your dog becomes less alert, even falls asleep on the down, it means he understands that he's not going anywhere until you say so, so he might as well get some shut-eye. This is good. He has learned how—and from whom—to learn.

Teaching your puppy how to learn first will not only speed basic obedience, but housebreaking as well. It can replace yelling and frustrating repetition. It's also a great way to find out just how smart your little guy really is.

The training method I like best copies the way dogs are able to transfer information and education from one to another. This natural communication can't be topped and communication is the essence of education. So if you want to learn how to communicate better with your dog, watch the way a mother canine communicates with her young. Like her, you can use sounds, gestures and touch to praise or correct a dog. Like her, you can make sure that praising activities encourage but clearly do not interrupt and that correcting activities discourage and clearly do interrupt. And finally, like the mother canine, never offer nor withhold food as a method of teaching. It makes the dog work for the food, instead of working to learn. Working with food rewards, you will never see the satisfaction and pride clearly visible when nothing is put between the learner and the learning.

Using this natural method of training, even the most recalcitrant learner can come to feel the satisfaction of mastering something new. His own good feeling, self-praise if you will, plus the added encouragement of your gentle verbal and physical praise, so like his mother's in quality and quantity, will eventually make for a happy, well-trained animal, one who can work with energy, zest and confidence, and, most important, one who will *want* to work for you.

6

The Well-Mannered Puppy

GOOD MANNERS are the key to a good, long-lasting relationship with your dog. The puppy who keeps the house clean, who never nips you, who doesn't chew your things, who knows when to be quiet and who won't jump all over everyone is the dog you'll live with—happily ever after. Good manners should begin in puppyhood. But they do not come automatically. You have to teach them. Here's how:

HOUSEBREAKING PUPPY

The number-one job you'll need to do is teach your puppy where to relieve himself. Housebreaking your puppy will be easier than you think. Watch:

1. Give it a name...

2. Use a crate and a schedule...

As he gets better, leave him out longer.

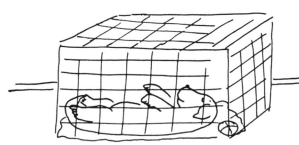

7 A.M. Food, water, walk*
Play 15-20 min.
Crate

11 A.M. Water, walk, play, crate

3 P.M. Food, water, walk
Play & train
Crate

7 P.M. Water, walk play, crate

11 P.M. Walk
Kiss
Crate overnight

*Walk to paper if too young to go out.

3. Remember to praise...

Some frequently asked questions about housebreaking

What should I do when my dog has an accident? If you catch your puppy in the act, interrupt him with a loud NO and take him right outside or to his papers. If you don't catch him, lead him (do not call him) to the scene of his crime, hit the floor (NOT THE PUPPY) so that he looks at his mess, tell him NO and take him right out or to his papers, using your buzz words (Hurry up, hurry up) and praise to remind and encourage him in the appropriate setting. After the walk, clean up immediately and well. Leaving accidents around gives the message that it's okay to mess indoors.

When your puppy has an accident, never hit him with a rolled up newspaper or anything else. Never rub his nose in his mess. These practices do not teach. They only frighten. And a frightened dog will not be in the frame of mind to learn anything from you.

What if I don't catch him in the act? Lead your puppy to the mess—he will know it's his by the scent—and proceed as above, saying NO, walking him, cleaning up well. Don't make a big fuss. Housebreaking is best handled with calm and vigilance.

How can I speed up my puppy's training? Teach the sit stay. It teaches your puppy to look at you, to listen and to take you seriously. Be consistent, always feeding your puppy and walking him at the same times each day. If he has accidents on the way out, carry him from crate to out of doors. This works wonders! Or, if he's too big to carry, heel him out. He's much less likely to have an accident if he's "working."

At what age will my dog be physically able to be reliable? Not before six months. But during all the months before that, he'll be better and better each week.

Where should I keep my puppy's crate? At night, the crate is in your bedroom so that your puppy does not have to sleep alone. During the day, move the crate to the kitchen or the family room, wherever you are. A puppy needs a lot of company. Remember—he's a pack animal.

TEACHING PUPPY NOT TO CHEW YOUR THINGS

You can also use the crate to prevent destructive chewing during your puppy's teething period and for several months afterward.

Monitor him when you are home, offering him a safe chew toy to gnaw on and correcting him by saying NO and giving him one tug on his collar when he starts to chew on anything of yours.

Do not give him socks and shoes to chew. He cannot tell the difference between one shoe and another and will chew your good shoes if you do this. Do not make a big deal over his chewing. If he moves from toy to molding, say NO and move him back away from the wall and to his chew toy, saying, "GOOD dog."

When you cannot watch your dog, be sure he's been outside to relieve himself and that he's had some good wholesome exercise—a romp in the yard, a long walk, play time with the kids, the chance to chase a ball—and then put him in his crate. Don't leave him in the crate all day long. Do use it for an hour or two at a time when no one will be able to watch the puppy to make sure he doesn't chew something dangerous to him or of value to you.

Gradually, as he grows up and gets obedience training, he will learn to chew his rawhide and toys and not your furniture and shoes. Meanwhile, remember this:

> The better he's trained, the less likely he is to indulge in destructive chewing.
>
> The better he's exercised, the less likely he is to chew your things. A tired dog is a good dog because a tired dog is a sleeping dog!
>
> The calmer he is—brush him, play with him, get him outside a lot—the less likely he is to chew destructively.

As you can see, destructive chewing is not an isolated problem. It is directly related to everything else in your dog's life.

As your puppy matures and gets educated, try giving him longer and longer periods of time out of the crate while you are at home. If he is good, begin to give him very short periods of freedom when you have to go out. Leave him out of the crate when you go for the mail or run around the corner for a quart of milk. If this works, gradually give him more time out of the crate, but don't be afraid to go back to square one if he gets destructive. In that case, take away his freedom temporarily, making sure you correct any destructive chewing he tries when you are home. In addition, go over all the other elements in his life.

> Is he getting enough attention, exercise, training, praise and correction?
>
> Are you expecting too much too soon from him?
>
> Is he lonely or bored? Try leaving the radio on when you go out.

Teaching him not to be destructive will take time, but, with training, by the time he's ten or twelve months old, he should be trustworthy.

TEACHING PUPPY TO BE QUIET

The easiest way to teach your puppy to be quiet when you need his silence is to teach him to bark on command. Here are six easy steps to get the job done.

1. Give it a name...

2. Practice when she's going to bark any way — the mailman is coming, someone is knocking on your door, she sees another dog...

3. Or bark to start her.

4. Practice every day for 1 or 2 minutes. Once she barks on command, The control is yours. Begin her with SPEAK...

5. Stop her when she barks inappropriately or for too long by saying ENOUGH and, if necessary, putting your hand under her collar and giving one tug. Praise immediately for silence.

6. Teach her a speaking trick (Chapter 8) so that she has a legitimate chance to use her voice.

c. benjamin
© 1990 arf

TEACHING PUPPY NOT TO JUMP UP

Lots of people love it when a cute dog jumps up on them. Lots of other people don't. That aside, it's not only annoying when a dog jumps up, it can be dangerous, too. A jumping dog won't hesitate to jump on little children or old people, or people wearing white silk or a tuxedo. Get the point? Your dog couldn't care less who his victim is. He's having fun.

The easiest way to correct this bad habit is to use a collar and leash and yank the dog straight back in mid-jump, using the verbal command NO JUMPING. Then ask him to sit and praise. Since it's attention he's after, giving him the attention while he's sitting will reenforce good manners while correcting the bad ones.

When company comes, snap the leash onto your dog's collar before you open the door. As his eyes open wide—*victims!*—and his front legs come off the ground, yank back as you say, NO JUMPING. Tell him SIT, and have your friends praise him as he stays sitting.

Some people have a hard time pulling straight back to make this correction. If you do, simply pull to the side and get him off balance and back on the floor. It's easier and works just as well.

When you are out for a walk, use the same correction if your dog tries to jump on people in the street. But be sure to be consistent. If it's sometimes yes and sometimes no, you'll run the risk of your dog jumping on one of those people who don't think it's so cute when a dog jumps on them and, your luck, it'll be a lawyer!

TEACHING YOUR PUPPY NEVER TO NIP

Puppies use their mouths when they play. You have already read about the importance of your dog growing up with his littermates (chapter 3). One important thing that happens in those first two months of play is that the puppies learn not to bite each other hard.

When nice dogs play, they may pretend to fight, jostling each other and grabbing legs, necks, tails, whatever. As long as they are having fun and not hurting each other, this is fine. After all, *they* have thick coats. But we have unprotected skins. So our dogs must learn never, ever to bite us, even in play. It is dangerous and foolhardy to allow a dog to nip at you or your clothes or bite you, even when he's young. He will grow and his bite will get stronger. He should not feel it is okay to put his teeth on a person—ever.

When your puppy nips you—and rest assured, he will—first tell him NO. If he nips again—and rest assured, he will—this time slip a finger under his collar and give one yank as you repeat NO. If he nips a third time, repeat the second correction and put him in his crate for thirty minutes to cool down. The message is, if *that's* the way you're going to play, you can't play with me.

It's perfectly normal for little puppies to nip. They must be taught not to. It will take you a few weeks to do this. As you do, the more *other* training you do, the better your puppy will listen and learn.

As you play with your puppy, never tease him or allow anyone else to. Never let him pull on your clothes or bite on your arm, either bare or wrapped in a towel. Those practices would encourage him to bite. And don't make the mistake of thinking that encouraging him to bite will make him more protective. It won't. It would only make him grow up wild, inappropriate, confused and dangerous. He'd be more likely to bite you than protect you. After all, what lesson did you really teach—to bite *your arm*.

A dog with strong pack loyalty, a dog who has a fair, humane leader, a benevolent alpha, *may* protect you if you need protection. Protecting the pack is part of being a dog. It has nothing whatsoever to do with "practicing" biting on his owner's arm or hands.

So when your puppy tries to nip you or anyone else, correct him with a strong NO, use a yank on his collar if necessary, work on his obedience training and always praise him for playing gently. When playing with *your* chosen puppy, play it smart.

NEUTERING YOUR PUPPY

Do you remember what you saw in the shelter when you went to select your puppy? There were lots and lots of other puppies, cute ones, sweet ones, funny ones, all without homes. In all likelihood, not all of those puppies were as lucky as yours. Not all of those puppies were adopted. Some were killed.

Each year in the United States, millions of unwanted dogs are killed because there are more of them than there are of us, people willing to give a dog a loving home. Don't add to this tragic overpopulation. Neuter your dog.

Unneutered Dog

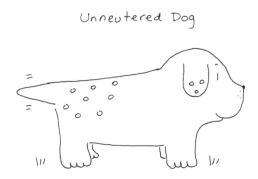

Here are some facts about neutering you ought to know:

Neutering your dog shows the world that you are a responsible person. It has no reflection whatsoever on your own sex life.

A neutered pet is easier to train, will concentrate better on you, is much less likely to fight with other dogs, is less pressured to mark territory with urine, both indoors and out, and has less desire to get away from you and roam.

Neutered dogs are not able to make unwanted puppies.

Neutered dogs do not get fat unless you overfeed them.

Neutered dogs are not less protective than unneutered dogs.

Neutered dogs make gentler, calmer pets.

Neutered dogs avoid certain health risks, such as pyometra (a life-threatening infection in females), and have a lower risk of other serious problems such as breast cancer in the female and prostate cancer in the male.

This aside, most shelters require the neutering of all adopted pets. If you are still not convinced, go back to the shelter and ask them to *show you* why they make this requirement.

HIS BUSINESS, YOUR BUSINESS

In these modern times of overpopulation, whether a dog can mate or not is not his business. It's yours. He's not a wild animal. He's a pet. He won't be able to care for his offspring himself. That would be your responsibility, so it's your business.

It's also your business if your dog focuses his sexuality on you. You should never let your dog mount you or any other person. Simply slip your hand under his collar, yank him sharply to the side, throwing him off balance and therefore off you, saying NO, and with your hand still in his collar, tell him to sit. Now praise.

What if your dog mounts another dog? Dogs often do this to express dominance. Little puppies do it in play, sometimes the female taking the male role. Unless the dog being mounted is tiny and in danger of being hurt, this is not your business. The dogs themselves will take care of this correction. Please note that once you neuter your dog, he will be less likely to show any sexual behavior.

If your dog licks himself, anywhere, that's his business, too. After all, he's just a dog. He needs manners, true, but not human ones. Don't worry about it when your dog cleans itself by licking. If a visitor is apt to be offended, you can simply distract the dog with a toy.

It is normal for a male dog's penis to extend beyond the sheath and be visible. Some people find this disturbing. But for a male dog, this is a normal reaction to any kind of excitement, even the excitement of a training lesson. So show *your* good manners, and let him be. After all, your dog is not a plastic flamingo, created to decorate your front lawn. One of the reasons you chose to live with an animal is that it would bring you closer to nature. That it will!

Good manners, taught early, will last a lifetime. By teaching some limits, by praising his good behavior, by correcting inappropriate behavior and by knowing what to correct and what to leave alone, you can raise a dog to be proud of. Now let's get on with the rest of his education.

7

The Obedient Puppy

OBEDIENCE TRAINING will help ensure your puppy's safety (he'll come when you call him, he'll walk close to your side, he'll stay when you tell him to) and your sanity (he'll come when you call him, he'll walk close to your side, he'll stay when you tell him to).

Obedience training will be fun for you and your puppy. Good training never breaks a dog's spirit, any more than his mother's praise and correction did. Instead, it will earn him more affection and freedom than he could safely have untrained.

By starting training early, your puppy will learn to do the right thing long before he gets into the habit of doing the wrong thing. This doesn't mean he'll never misbehave. After all, he's going to be an adolescent one day. He's going to have to do his share of testing, just to see *for sure* how things stand. He's a dog. So even after he's an adult, it's normal for him to see, every once in a while, if he can move up in the pecking order. At those times, you'll have his training to fall back on. Your answer to his question can be a thirty-minute down stay, a little tune-up of all his training, even just a firm NO accompanied by some serious eye contact. None of this will break his spirit. It will simply demonstrate, again, that even though much of your teaching is done via games, you are more than capable of being firm when it's necessary. Knowing you're in charge, knowing how to behave and knowing how to please you will help your pup to be a more spirited fellow for all of his life.

You have already taught your puppy the sit stay (chapter 5). If not, please do this now because this is how your puppy learns how to learn. Next, let's show your puppy the great advantage of coming when he's called. And just to prove we mean it when we say training will be fun, we'll teach these games via cartoons!

RECALL GAMES

Puppy, come!

1. Call your puppy...

2. Praise him for coming.

* Practice every day.

Catch me if you can—and you can!

1. Run away...

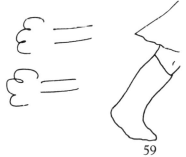

2. Let him catch you.

Good, smart, fast puppy!

benjamin

Hide and seek.

1. Hide in a silly place and call, whistle or squeak a squeak toy...

2. Praise when he finds you...

And finally, come and sit.

1. Put your puppy on a sit stay, back away, wait, then call him to come.

2. When he gets close, tell him <u>sit</u> and praise when he does.

Sit ... G<u>OO</u>D puppy!

C.benjamin

What if your puppy doesn't come when you call him? Easy! Go and get him, put on his leash and practice sit stay, come, sit stay, come 10 times in a row. (Don't forget the praise!)

Come

Another one?!! I'll never be bad again.

← ← tug, tug if necessary...

Some tips to remember.

Never call your puppy for something he will view as negative. It will make him *not* come when called. When you want to correct your puppy, cut his nails, give him a bath, confine him, go and get him.

WHEN YOU TRAIN YOUR PUPPY, NEVER YELL AT HIM, YOU HEAR?

Never hit your puppy. Use a tug on his collar and a sharp NO instead.

DOWN STAY

Here is how to teach your puppy to lie down on command:

Week 1

1. Pat the floor, saying <u>Down</u>...

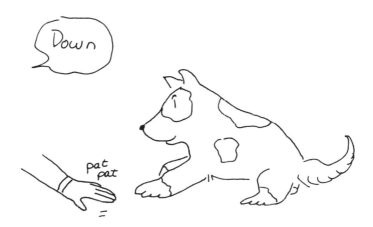

Or slide the puppy's legs forward.

2. Gently roll the puppy over and rub his belly.

C. benjamin
© 1990

*Practice every day for a week.

Week 2

1. Pat the floor and say <u>down</u>.

2. Put the leash over his back, tell him <u>stay</u> and slowly back away.

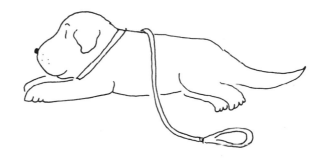

3. Wait... then call him to come.

Puppy, puppy, come, sweetheart

And praise!

More tips.

Increase the time of the down stay in variable order—one minutes, five minutes, two minutes, eight minutes, fifteen minutes and so on—until your puppy will do a long down, staying for thirty minutes at a time without breaking. This should take about three to four weeks of practice. And, yes, *he* may fall asleep on the down stay, but no, *you* may not. You have to stay in the room and awake to make sure that he doesn't just get up and leave and so that, when the time comes, you can break him with an OKAY and praise.

Never break a command because you see that your puppy is about to do just that. You know who you are! And so does he!

Train when you are in a good mood.

Train the puppy *before* he eats, not after.

Always end each session with a little game—hide and seek, catch me if you can, come and pounce (all in this chapter), retrieving, catching (in chapter 8).

HEEL

When you take your puppy out, he needs some slack on the leash so that he can investigate, sniff around, relieve himself. After he gets a few minutes to do just that, you should have him heel. This means he will walk at your left side, at your pace, starting and stopping when you do.

Heeling may be the most difficult thing you teach your puppy. It will almost surely take the most time. After all, he must adjust his movement to yours while yours is changing. So it will take him a while to catch on.

In addition to the fact that heeling is difficult to teach and to learn, your puppy will be easily distracted while he is out of doors. He will want to sniff everything and to change direction at whim. This is exactly why sanity demands you teach him to heel.

Walking at your side, he'll be safer. Walking nicely, he'll be an easy companion, so you will take him out more often and for longer walks. Even if you have a large fenced yard in which he can play and relieve himself, he needs to get out into the larger world away from home in order for him to become and remain a socialized, well-balanced dog. So, he must learn to heel.

1. With the puppy sitting at your left, pat your left leg, say puppy, heel and step out with your left foot. (The puppy follows the leg he's closest to.)

"Puppy? Heel"

"♪♪" pat pat

2. If he lags or forges ahead, pat your leg and say _heel_ as you tug and release so that he's back in place.

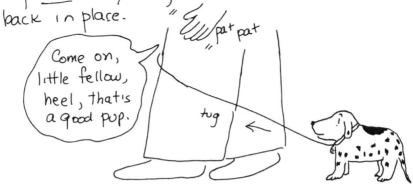

Come on, little fellow, heel, that's a good pup.

pat pat

tug

* Encourage him as you go along.

3. If he forges ahead like a maniac, turn and change direction. This will give him a bigger tug — more motivation to pay attention.

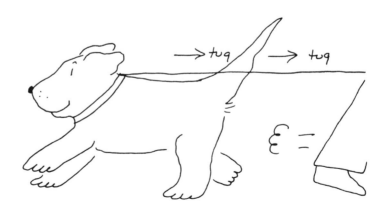

→ tug   → tug

4. Have him sit when you stop.

Good boy!

* Practice every day!

Surprise!

Surprise the puppy several times a week when he's heeling. Still holding the leash, but allowing slack, break away and run a couple of steps from him saying, "Puppy, come, come, come." Crouch and let him pounce on you. Then praise and resume heeling.

Stop walking and have the puppy sit at your left side. Tell him to stay, using the hand signal. Walk forward toward the end of the leash (right foot moves first when he's *not* coming with you) and just before the leash gets taut, pat your leg, say, "Puppy, heel," and keep going. The puppy should rush to catch up, then slow to your pace. Praise warmly in motion.

Always give your puppy an "Okay" and a slack leash at the end of the walk as well as at the beginning. A young pup may easily need to relieve himself again at the end of a fifteen-minute outing. He will surely need to investigate again.

Don't forget—there is hardly another thing on earth as sweet as a puppy! So have fun as you train, practice and play! For more ways to have fun with puppies, try the next chapter.

8

Advanced Learning for Puppies

THERE'S MORE to dog training than obedience work. There are other things you can teach your dog, things that will make him smarter, more attentive, easier to exercise, more fun.

FUN RETRIEVING

It's natural for a puppy to chase and "capture" a tempting, moving object. Here are the steps that will turn this instinct into a game.

1. Tease

2. Toss

3. Encourage

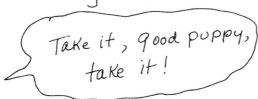

Take it, good puppy, take it!

crinkle

4. Call

Puppy, Come

crinkle

5. Retrieve

Out!
Good puppy.

Crinkle

C. benjamin
© 1990

✗ If he doesn't drop the object, open his mouth, take it and praise warmly, as if he did it on his own.

Tips

Heighten interest in the object by hiding it behind you, tossing it in the air and catching it, shaking it.

In order to keep this a fun game, do not retrieve the "prize" from the puppy every time. Sometimes let the puppy keep it. He may bring it to you on his own after he gets to play with it for a while. When he does, praise and play again.

When retrieving the object from the puppy, *never* pull or tug on it while it is in his mouth. That would teach the puppy to hold on even tighter and not give up objects he is holding.

Play indoors and out, in fenced areas. Use many different objects—balls, toys, sticks, crinkled paper.

FIND IT!

Once the puppy knows his sit stay pretty well, add this finding game. You'll love this game because it's not only fun, it also reenforces your puppy's training. He'll love it because he gets to use his nose and,

73

in the beginning, he gets a little snack when he "wins." Later on, winning alone will be enough to keep him happy.

1. Put puppy on a sit stay and let him smell the biscuit...

Smell it!

2. Place the biscuit 2 feet away...

Staaay...

3. After 4 seconds...

4. Praise as he devours his prize ...

Gradually move the prize farther away. If the puppy is playing the game well (staying until the release word, finding the biscuit right away, having a good time), by the end of week one, the biscuit can be in the doorway to the next room. During week two, hide the biscuit just beyond the doorway. By week three, you can hide the biscuit farther into the next room, then on a step or low shelf, finally, on the bed, on a table (as long as he can reach it!), in your pocket. If at any time the puppy has trouble finding the biscuit, help him by walking near where you hid it, saying, "Find it, good dog, find it," and go back to some easier finds for him. He must succeed in order to like the game. Once he's good at it, switch the prize to a ball, a toy, a set of keys, a stick, a handkerchief and, every once in a while, a biscuit.

BARK MY AGE

You have already taught your puppy to bark on command (chapter 6). Now you can use that useful command, SPEAK, to help you teach your puppy one intriguing trick and one hilarious trick. Dogs love doing tricks because they love to make people laugh.

Intriguing trick: Add.

1.

2.

Hilarious trick: Bark my age.

1.

GO TO YOUR PLACE

Will *your* chosen puppy ever be a pest? I dare say he will, but not for long. If you teach him to go to his place, you can send him to lie down whenever you've had enough.

Make a place for your puppy with a mat, a sheepskin, an old towel. In this way, your puppy's place will be portable and you can have him go to his place when appropriate at home and away. He can even have his place in the car.

1. Give the command...

GO TO YOUR PLACE

C. benjamin
© 1990

2. Run your puppy to his mat.

Down, good pup.

pat pat

c.benjamin

* Practice until he can make the trip on his own.

CATCH IT

Most dogs are notoriously poor at catching objects until they learn the knack through practice. Initially, motivate this game by tossing a small piece of dog biscuit right at his muzzle, after letting him smell it. And don't fret if it bounces off his face the first ten times. He'll catch on.

1. Practice...

2. Practice...

Tips

In the beginning, let him eat whatever you throw, even if he misses. Once he starts catching, only let him eat what he actually catches in his mouth.

After he catches well, switch to a ball. After he catches the ball with a satisfying thud, call him, tell him OUT, back away and play again.

THE IMPORTANCE OF PLAY

Play is important as a learning tool, but it is also important in itself. The tricks, games and routines you have taught your puppy will help you spend time together and enjoy each other. These easy routines will help you exercise your puppy as he grows. Play increases the communication between the players. It tightens the bond between person and dog. And a round of games after school or work will help ease the tension for both of you.

Tricks and games are also a great way to show off your best friend, to your other best friends, to people you meet as you take long walks or, if you choose to volunteer, to people in institutions who cannot have a dog of their own. Trained, well mannered, socialized, well versed in tricks and games, your dog can go anywhere. Think about it!

9

Growing Up Canine

MOST OF US have goals for our dogs—a nice, obedient pet, a companion for the children, an alarm dog to bark when someone comes, someone to come home to, a bed warmer, a therapy dog, a movie star. But your dog has an existence separate from his life as your pet. Before everything else, he is a dog, has a right and need to be a dog, can't be anything but a dog, and as such, he has the inalienable right to grow up canine.

He has a right to have his natural language understood. Aside from teaching him English (sit, stay, down, come, do you want this? and more), you should speak canine—not just understand it, but speak it. You should know the meaning of all his gestures, facial expressions, body language and sounds, those endemic to dogs in general, those specific to your own dog. You should sometimes imitate these gestures in order to communicate with your dog in his own tongue. He has a need and right to be understood, as all living creatures do.

He has a right to natural structure in his life. He needs some order to his pack, a clear leader, a clear pecking order, some consistency. This gives him a sense of order in the universe, a sense that his world is understandable and clear. This allows him to know how to proceed. It makes him secure and comfortable in a way that always getting his way cannot.

He has a right to education. He has a mind and a desire to use it. He is born, as we are, with curiosity and intelligence. His life will be richest if he can use both to the maximum. Your bonus—educated, he'll be an infinitely more interesting companion.

He has a right to education...

Do you have a sporting type dog and no desire to hunt, a herding type mix and no flock, a sight hound cross and no desert filled with game? No matter. When you can't help your dog live out his genetic heritage by teaching him that which he was bred to do—haul a sled, move the sheep, protect your estate, bring a downed duck to hand— you can expand or alter your dog's potential instead by dipping into his specific talents (retrieving, guarding, herding) and the general talents of his species (tracking, scent discrimination, obedience work, agility work). You can give him work around the house and in your neighborhood (collecting twigs in the yard, collecting laundry in the house, carrying packages from the store, sounding the alarm when someone comes). You can make him the ambassador of good cheer, teaching him sociable tricks (give your paw, find an object hidden on a person, speak, whine, howl on command) and having him entertain your family and friends or, if time permits, people in institutions such as nursing homes, hospitals, rehabilitation centers and homes for the mentally or physically handicapped. There are jobs to be done that any dog can apply himself to and be the better dog for it.

He has a right to use what he's got. He has a body, muscles, energy. He must flex himself. He must move. Insufficient exercise is one of the underlying causes of many dog problems. Simply stated, the more energy your dog uses up constructively, the less energy he'll have available to use up destructively. He needs more than running around. He needs some planned exercise to increase confidence, agility, speed, strength and stamina, especially if you have big plans for him—to be well trained, terrific with kids, a real clown, a therapy dog, a great pet.

He has a right to privacy. There are times he may just want to be left alone. Every creature needs time to rest, adjust, be alone, time to integrate what he has learned, time to go blank and do nothing, time just to be.

He has a right to the company of his own species. Yes, he loves you. No, that is not enough. Only another dog can understand him and play with him in a perfectly smooth way with no communication glitches, with no physical awkwardness.

He has a right to be protected. He must see his veterinarian regularly for a check-up and proper inoculations. He needs protection from the elements—excessive heat and cold. He needs a warm, dry place to sleep. He needs a wholesome diet, appropriate to his age and size, and a supply of fresh, clean water. He needs someone—you— who will consider his needs at least for a small part of every day.

He has a right to be leashed or fenced or, at the very least, accompanied when he goes out. He cannot understand what a car could do to him. There are no car-smart dogs, only drivers with quick instincts and good brakes. Running "free," he could pack up with other dogs and, gaining confidence from numbers, attack other animals or even people. The nicest dog in the world is still a pack animal. (He's a dog, isn't he?) He could knock over garbage cans and kill himself eating chicken bones. He could get lost, stolen or killed. Your chosen puppy should never go out without a responsible human companion to keep him safe.

He has a right to be disciplined. He is a dog. It is a natural, understandable, important part of being a dog to learn from and get order through both positive and negative reenforcement, whether that comes from you or from another dog. Think of his mother. Yes—she petted and cleaned him with her smooth tongue, she cooed to him, she nuzzled him, she let him sleep near the considerable warmth of her body. But she also growled and snarled at him when he was in danger, cheeky or out of line in any way. She also slammed him with her paw or rolled him on his back when his behavior needed editing. She was swift, fair and graceful. Her communication was always perfect. She never had to repeat herself a second time. This is part of a dog's natural life—praise and correction, rewards and punishment, positive and negative reenforcement. It doesn't matter to the dog what you call it. It only matters that it is part and parcel of what makes life comfortable and clear for a dog.

He has a right to be loved. Don't we all? He needs to be fondled, cuddled and stroked, to be told he's wonderful. He needs smiles, pats, approval, treats. Isn't that one of the reasons you adopted him, to always have someone to hug?

He has a right to be loved.

And saddest of all to have to say, **he has the right not to be subjected to pain and torture,** nor be held captive in an unloving and fearful place, nor to be the subject of experiments nor live a hopeless life and die when his caretakers have finished using him. He has a right not to be regarded as less than we are just because he cannot speak for himself. Anyone who lets himself truly know a dog will know he is not less, just different.

In all his various shapes and sizes, he is magnificent to behold— loyal and funny, graceful and touching, natural, smart, mysterious, important. There's not much around as perfect as the dog.

You have chosen one to be your special friend. You have worked hard to socialize, civilize and train him. Now, and for as long as he lives, enjoy!

Afterword

If you enjoyed this book and would like to learn more about your dog, you might like some of the other books by this author.

For more on raising and training puppies: *Mother Knows Best, The Natural Way to Train Your Dog.*

For children ten and up: *Dog Training for Kids.*

Should a problem arise: *Dog Problems.*

For fun and games: *Dog Tricks: Teaching Your Dog to Be Useful, Fun and Entertaining.*

If you'd like to adopt a dog five months old or older: *Second-Hand Dog: How to Turn Yours Into a First-Rate Pet.*

Obedience classes are also highly recommended—a puppy class for dogs under five months of age, an obedience training class for dogs over five months of age. Class is informative, effective, social and fun, a wonderful way to train your chosen puppy.